THE BEST POSTERS OF 1946

1946

POSTER GALLERY

SELECTED BY J I BIEGELEISEN

NEW YORK
REENBERG : PUBLISHER

FOREWORD

You will want to know something about this, the first issue of *Poster Gallery:* what its scope is, how the work that appears here was selected, and who did the selecting. You will no doubt also be interested in the criteria of evaluation that governed the final choice.

To answer these questions in their proper sequence, *Poster Gallery* is an ambitious project undertaken by a Committee of One who is thoroughly familiar with what passes as poster art in America and whose critical viewpoint toward it is shared by the majority of artists who practice the profession. They are resentful and critical of the system of mass advertising which has robbed them of their liberty to do something original.

Want to design a poster? It's easy. Here's the community formula guaranteed to be acceptable in any part of the country. Select a slogan, pun, rhyme, jingle, or any inane play on words. Get a realistic illustration to match. Some of the prop figures to choose from are a cooing baby, a talking dog or any other expressive animal endowed with human qualities, a freckly nosed boy, an embarrassing situation. When in doubt, show a charming girl with a seductive smile and a low-cut dress—regardless of the product you are selling. Finish off this composition with the client's favorite logotype placed conspicuously on the poster, and whenever possible make room for the trademark, no matter whether you think the design is a monstrosity or a masterpiece. There you have it. Send the art work to the lithographer and get it plastered all over town. On billboards and panels; on the highways; in the interiors of subways, busses, and trolleys; on the sides of passing trucks; on walls; in shop windows. The new poster replaces the old, but it makes hardly any difference.

I have yet to speak to an artist who has offered a word of praise for the American formula of poster design. Occasionally I meet up with an art director, who has long ago ceased to be creative, who will defend this type of poster advertising on the ground that the poster sells the product and "that's what counts." Even from his hard commercial point of view—forgetting art for art's sake—there is a flaw in this argument in favor of mediocrity. It may be pointed out that the advertiser would get even more for his money if his poster were made to look different from his competitor's on the adjacent panel. Thus, by giving the artist more latitude in creative expression, not only would the artist be a happier man (which is only incidental), but the client could be happier, too. And so ends a sermon which has been preached from many an art pulpit.

As to the scope of *P.G.* Here the endeavor has been to collect the best posters that have been produced during the current year, under conditions as they are today. The work that appears in *P.G.* has been selected from four hundred of the best designs submitted from all parts of the United States. The designers whose work is represented here were approached either personally or through their agents or agencies. Each one was invited to submit his favorite designs produced during the current year, and from this aggregate total, about eighty posters were finally picked. While it was my original intention to select one hundred American posters, I found that I could not follow through on this plan because I could not find one hundred which could honestly be classified under "the best posters of the year." To make up this deficit I hit upon an idea which has its compensations. I have included about twenty of the best foreign posters produced during the past few years. This series seems so worthwhile that I plan to include a permanent section of European posters in all future issues of *Poster Gallery*.

In appointing myself a one-man committee, I know very well that I am sticking my neck out—so my best friends tell me. I have thrown caution to the winds because it is my sincere conviction that making a personal selection is the most expedient and direct approach to the problem. I am, comparatively speaking, a free agent— free to express my choice without concessions and without restraint, since I owe no allegiance to account executives, clients, or front-office bigwigs whose special favors I might want to curry.

As to the basis or criteria of judging these posters. In one of my previous books, *Poster Design*, there appeared a chapter entitled "What Makes a Poster Click?" In it, I outline the cardinal principles of design—the principles that guided me in making the selections that appear in this annual. I have taken the liberty of transcribing that chapter so that my basis for selection will be fully understood.

All of the posters submitted to me were carefully studied as to their relative merits, were discussed and argued about with others; but the final decision rested with me. Not all the work shown here conforms in every way to my standards of good poster design. Nor does this compilation necessarily include the only good posters which were done this past year in America. The selection merely represents the best of those posters that were sent to me for consideration by artists and agencies. And this is a narrowing limitation for several reasons. In the first place, I daresay that I did not contact every possible source for samples of poster work.

Then, too, many of those contacted were taking their vacations at the time the notice reached them and will someday (when they reach the bottom of the backlog pile of summer mail) come upon the invitation to participate. That indicates two excluded categories of possible entries. There is still a third. A few agencies, lacking in the pioneer spirit, hesitated to submit work for the first issue, and expressed a preference to "come in" when the annual has been more securely established.

It is for this reason that I am particularly grateful to all those who so heartily assisted in this venture by encouraging the project from its inception, by ransacking their studio files for the best material, by preparing special photographs, and by making many valuable suggestions:

Eugene P. Beitler of Pan American World Airways System; Lucien Bernhard; Joseph Binder; Austin Brew of B.B.D. & O.; Martin W. Carrick of Ketterlinus Lithographing Company; Edward F. Cauley of Cecil and Presbrey, Inc.; Helen Cornthwaite of British Information Service; F. A. Elsey of McCann-Erickson, Inc.; Roberto Fontaino of Information Bureau of Uruguay; Walter B. Geoghegan of Calkins and Holden; Dorothy Hall of Canadian National Film Board; Alfred B. Halpairn, Jr. of Einson-Freeman Company; George F. Held of Scandinavian Airlines System; A. Heppenheimer of British Information Service; Louis Honig of Honig-Cooper Company; Harry J. Jacknick of Harry J. Jacknick Company, Inc.; Marie Jessup of Children's Book Council; McKnight Kauffer; Addis F. Kean of Clements Company; M. B. Kelly of Maxon, Inc.; Herman Kornblum of Lawrence C. Gumbinner Agency; Morton Levin of Topps Chewing Gum; Jackson Lowell; Charles E. Mahony of Buchanan Advertising; May Marcus of National Council of American-Soviet Friendship; Mitchel Mark of Adam Hat Stores, Inc.; Raymond Martin of Consolidated Edison Company of New York; Sascha Maurer; C. D. McCormick of Outdoor Advertising Incorporated; Jules Menghetti of J. M. Mathes, Inc., E. F. Molyneux of Newell-Emmett Company; Eric Nice of The Joseph Katz Company; Paul Rand; Alan Randall of The Best Foods, Inc.; Betty Rhodes of American Airlines System; Mark Seelan of Outdoor Advertising Incorporated; Jack Skolnik of Pedlar and Ryan, Inc.; Paul Smith of D'Arcy Advertising Company; Harold A. Speckman of McCandlish Lithograph Corporation; Myles Standish of Standish, Inc.; Alex Steinweiss; Vincent Trotta of National Screen Service; J. B. Verlot of French National Railroads; Ward Baking Company; H. L. Webster of Wm. Wrigley Jr. Company; Arthur Werback of Abraham and Straus; W. E. Whited of J. Walter Thompson Company; Thomas M. Willis of Tooker Lithograph Company; Hamilton Wright.

J. I. Biegeleisen

WHAT MAKES A POSTER CLICK?

While there is no empirical way to evaluate the merit of a poster design (unless we refer to its tabulated effect on sales or some other equally calculable response), there are certain recognized requisites or principles of good poster design which must be followed to make a poster "click." In the critical analysis of a poster one should consider how many of these guiding principles the artist has incorporated in his design and how successfully he has done so.

THE CARDINAL PRINCIPLES OF POSTER DESIGN

SIMPLICITY

The layout should be simple. Generally speaking, the fewer units into which a given space is divided, the more pleasing it is to the eye. A poster should not be too busy. We often see posters which present a bewildering spectacle of confusing elements. It is as if the designer labored under the theory that if a few elements or units were good, then a good many of them must be so much better. If one illustration or panel is impressive, then why not put in three or four? This is not unlike the reasoning of a spectacular theatrical producer who, when he saw an early rehearsal of his pageant production of "The Last Supper," asked the director for twenty-four Apostles instead of twelve—to make it really "colossal."

A fussy conglomeration of units, needless to stress, entirely defeats the purpose of the poster. The best posters are those in which the units are few and simple. It is much better to have one large illustration dominate the composition, than to have a group of smaller ones compete with each other for attention. The lettering too should be kept within bounds. If placed within a panel, the shape of the panel should be kept simple and in harmony with the other shapes in the composition. Not everyone possesses the talent to make a poster technically perfect, but one need not be particularly gifted to make it simple; one must only resist the temptation to complicate it.

The treatment should be simple. Not only should the layout represent a simple division of space, but each unit in turn should by its simplicity add to the singleness of effect. There should be a minimum of different painting techniques and of different lettering styles. Copy should be logically separated into thought groups and arranged in block units. Feature wording, by its size and placement, should be given prominence over incidental copy. Only when that which is unimportant is subdued, does the featured copy stand out prominently by comparison.

A simple and organized arrangement with few elements, techniques, and lettering styles will make even a heavily-worded poster tolerably easy to read.

UNITY

Unity is the relationship or kinship between the several elements of a composition. The various elements that comprise a layout must seem part of the same poster; they must hold together. There are several ways of getting unity on a poster.

Direct overlapping of elements. The most direct way to knit the elements together is to make one touch or overlap the other. The illustration is often made to overlap or extend into a line of lettering. When there are four or five elements in the design and it is not possible to have them touch at some point, some other unifying device must be used.

Pointing Devices. An artificial device may be introduced to bridge the channels separating the component elements in a composition. Some of the most obvious ways of directing the visual flow that develop unity are the arrow, the pointing finger, the decorative dots or rules and other devices borrowed from the typographer's bag of tricks. Sometimes the flourishing tail of a letter is artfully extended to lasso a roaming unit in a composition. In these ways the eye is guided rhythmically from one element to another, so that the design is encompassed as a whole.

We are all familiar with the design where the advertised product is used as a pointing device. The fountain pen or pencil is aimed in the direction of the trade name or selling price; oil or some other liquid is shown flowing from a source at the top of the advertisement, down in a long unifying stream to the bottom where the company's name appears. Cough drops or pills are made to drop out of a container and in their descent, lead the eye over a prescribed course to the brand name.

Unity may be attained by making two elements of the design face or incline towards each other or in some other way optically span the gap between distant though related units. In a formal type of poster, where the elements of the layout are presented in a sequential arrangement without touching, overlapping, or pointing to each other, a strong border will help to convey a feeling of unity to the composition.

BALANCE

A poster may have unity without having balance, if the elements on one side are unified by one of the means described above, but if there are none on the other side to balance the combined weight. There are two kinds of balance: formal and informal. A wet ink spot on a piece of paper folded in half, will result in an accidental design that is perfectly matched—truly bisymmetric. In a poster based on such formal balance, an imaginary axis running through the center will divide the design so that one half will represent the mirrored reflection of the other. A composition based on formal balance is static and always safe. It suggests repose, tranquility, contemplation, but no action. It is decorative, but not dynamic, and does not motivate the onlooker to do anything because it does not do anything itself. When the artist strives for classic atmosphere and stability, a layout based on bisymmetric balance will best transmit that feeling.

Balance is really a matter of creating an equilibrium so that what is on one side of the seesaw will somehow equal what is on the other side. To convey a feeling of balance without resorting to "blotto" symmetry requires imagination and daring on the part of the artist. He must employ color, strategic placement of copy or illustration, typographical devices and other means to equalize the forces. Informal balance, alternately referred to as occult or asymmetric balance, is dynamic in its appeal and is therefore more in keeping with the attention-getting objective of a poster.

THE SELLING POINT

The aim of a poster is to sell something—a product, a service, or a cause—and the aim should be clear. A poster should lead to action—immediate or eventual. The plan by which one hopes to reach this objective constitutes the idea or the selling point around which the copy and design of the poster are planned. The idea may be blunt; it may be expressed in a layout that is nothing more than a "blow-up" of the product, with copy which simply states, "Buy——," or "Ask for ——," or "Accept no substitute for ——." Such bluntness or naïveté is impotent because it does not tell *why* the potential customer should do as he is told or how he would benefit by following the command.

A good poster, once it has buttonholed the man in the street, rewards him in some way for the time it has demanded of him. The reward may be in the form of entertaining him through a humorous situation, it may instruct him by presenting an interesting bit of information, or it may put him in a good frame of mind by flattering his vanity. So the idea of an ad may hinge upon a popular saying, a play on words, a slogan, a rhyme, an anecdotal or dramatic situation, or merely a convincing statement of fact. However it may be presented, the idea or selling point should be perfectly clear.

SURPRISE

We were going to say that if a poster is to be the right kind of selling agent, it must deliver its message in some unusual and surprising manner. But then, every poster need not be a super-salesman. There are occasions when the tipping of his hat brings a salesman more results than a forceful slap on the shoulder. Institutional posters, through which the advertiser builds up good will and prestige by slow degrees, must, to add confidence to the message, exercise great restraint in their general tone, yet they play a big part in the promotion of the company's products.

When a poster is planned for a one-look audience, it must be made to attract attention to itself instantly. This can be done by some rousing element of surprise, so that even the casual passer-by will be jolted into taking another look. A dynamic poster stimulates an immediate emotional response by means of an aggressive color scheme, dramatic perspective, provoking layout, or unusual painting technique. There must be something new or startling.

A humorous or dramatic incident may be sufficient to attract attention. An anecdotal situation may be presented through the medium of a photograph, an illustration, cartoon, or symbolic design. The theme or subject matter may range from the ridiculous to the sublime. A typical example: a scene showing a hen-pecked husband who has made a night of it, stealthily sneaking upstairs in the wee hours of the morning. In his anxiety to get up there unnoticed, he fails to notice the cat which is asleep directly in his path. The beholder, by being made to participate in the action, will pause to survey the ad more completely.

Anything seen at eye level is not as interesting as the same thing viewed from an unusual vantage point, so a poster with its illustration drawn in some out-of-the-ordinary perspective, will evoke more surprise than one where the illustration is of a normal eye view. This urge to see the world from a different angle is inherent in human nature. It can be observed in the antics of children who take a curious delight in bending down to look through their outstretched legs at a topsy-turvy world. It has been taken into account by the motion picture industry which has developed the technique of the close-up, the long shot, the bird's-eye view, the snail's view, oblique view—any angle or view which dramatically departs from normal perspective.

Correlated with the idea of surprising perspective, is the matter of size. It is far more interesting to view things which are reduced to Lilliputian proportions or are fantastically enlarged. Size is relative. We measure one thing by comparing it with another. To give the impression of largeness or grandeur to a specific part of a design, one should contrast it with another part, exaggeratedly tiny. Another way of giving the illusion of colossal proportions is to focus attention on a magnified detail or fragment of an object instead of showing it in its entirety. It's a trick so to relate the dramatic detail to the composition that the detail seems to be larger than the poster itself.

Anything that suggests precarious or temporary balance immediately creates tension and suspense. We watch the tightrope walker's act with animated interest because we cannot help but participate mentally in his attempt to challenge the forces of equilibrium. We are somewhat similarly affected by a poster layout where the lettering or illustration is slanted dynamically and forcefully. The observer is more inclined to reach out mentally to something tilted than to a package or product firmly planted on its base.

The element of surprise in a poster may be wrought also by a painting technique or style that is surprisingly new and different. The typographical technique of an artist like Lester Beall is as refreshing as it is unique. The photomontage style of Herbert Matter will for a time (until it becomes public property through imitation), continue to attract attention.

WORKMANSHIP

Though it is difficult to say how much a superior painting technique contributes to the success of a poster, it is a definite fact that most people are agreeably affected by a piece of work that is well rendered. By rendering, we do not mean to include the idea or the layout. We limit our consideration here to the quality of workmanship judged from a perfectionist point of view. Is the artist a master of his medium? Is he a good designer and draftsman? Is he an expert letterer? To sum it all up, is he a skilled technician?

It is understood that the individual elements comprising a poster may be rendered beautifully without adding up to anything. Unless there is an idea behind it, a poster may be all dressed up but get nowhere. Conversely, a poster may have all other qualities—idea, simplicity, balance, unity, and surprise—but if the quality of workmanship is poor, the poster may be ineffectual. The ideal poster (and there are very few that fall into that category) possesses all six of the cardinal requisites mentioned in this chapter. Let us bear these criteria in mind in studying the collection of posters which appear in this book.

AMERICAN POSTERS

Give with your heart!

The non-sectarian **Community Committee** of New York

on behalf of The **United Jewish Appeal**

to help survivors overseas

artist LUCIEN BERNHARD ■ art director LUCIEN BERNHARD ■ agency S. A. LEAGUE COMPANY
■ client MARLBORO SHIRT COMPANY

Books are Bridges

BOOK WEEK
NOVEMBER 10-16 1946

MAUD-MISKA PETERSH

artist MAUD-MISKA PETERSHAM ■ client CHILDREN'S BOOK COUN

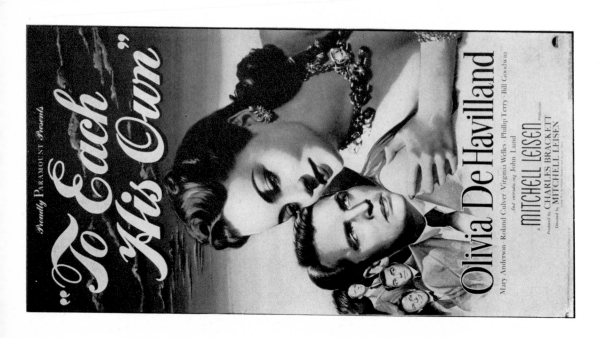

For Satisfying Quality -
be sure it's Wrigley's

WRIGLEY'S
SPEARMINT
CHEWING GUM

artist OTIS SHEPARD ■ art director OTIS SHEPARD ■ client WM. WRIGLEY JR. COMPANY

"certainly gives you a start!"

ESSO EXTRA GASOLINE

23

artist ALEX STEINWEISS ■ art director ALEX STEINWEISS ■ client COLUMBIA RECORDING CORPORATION

artist PAUL RAND ■ art director PAUL RAND ■ agency WM. H. WEINTRAUB & COMPANY ■ client CRESTA BLANCA WINE COMPANY

RKO presents...

Till the End of Time

Starring

Dorothy McGuire and Guy Madison

Robert Mitchum · Bill Williams

with Tom Tully · William Gargan · Jean Porter
Johnny Sands · Loren Tindall
A Dore Schary Production
Directed by Edward Dmytryk
Screen Play by Allen Rivkin

RKO RADIO

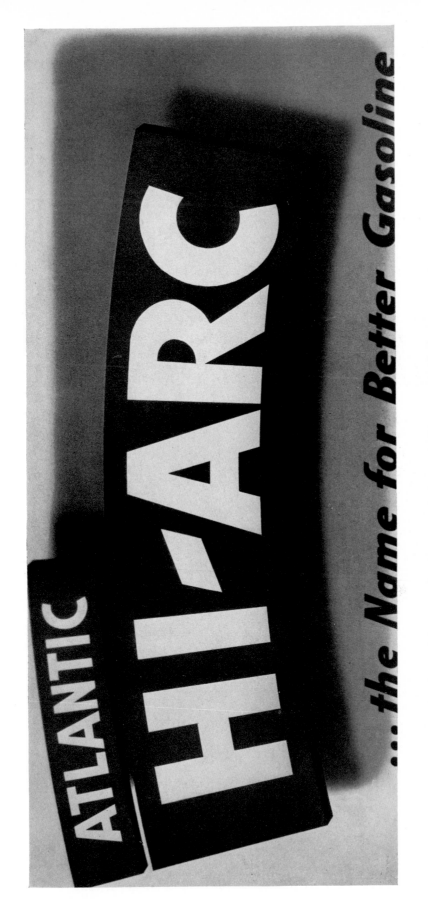

ATLANTIC **HI-ARC**

...the Name for Better Gasoline

artist CARL PAULSON ■ art director CARL EICHMAN ■ agency BENJ. ESHLEMAN COMPANY ■ client ATLANTIC REFINING COMPANY

artist POTTER-ZIEGLER ■ art director S. A. WELLS and W. C. SCOTT ■ agency McCANN-ERICKSON, INC.
■ client STANDARD OIL COMPANY-INDIANA

artist NAT WHITE ■ art director WALTER GEOGHEGAN ■ agency CALKINS & HOLDEN ■ client GULF OIL CORPORATION

KEEP YOUR SUBWAYS CLEAN

DEPOSIT
WASTE
PAPER

BATT

■ artist FRANK BATTIFARANO
■ art director JEFFERSON TESTER
■ client BOARD OF TRANSPORTATION

■ artist PATTERSON & HALL
■ art director FRED GLAUSER
■ agency HONIG-COOPER COMPANY
■ client WINE GROWERS GUILD

artist CARL PAULSON ■ art director LEON H. FOLLETT ■ agency STANDISH INC.
■ client NARRAGANSETT BREWING COMPANY

artist MARTINO BROTHERS ■ art director AZIO MARTINELLI ■ agency N. W. AYER & SON
■ client MICHIGAN BELL

artist WALTON S. THOMPSON ■ art director STANLEY F. SQUIRE ■ agency THE CLEMENTS COMPANY, INC.
■ client HORN AND HARDART

artist JOSEPH BINDER ■ art director E. EYERLY ■ agency BOTSFORD, CONSTANTINE & GARDNER ■ client JANTZEN KNITTING MILLS

■ artist ALEX STEINWEISS

■ art director ROBERT NELSON

■ client SCHENLEY DISTILLERS CORPORATION

artist ROBERT E. HARRIS ■ art director HENRY J. PAYNE ■ agency BATTON, BARTON, DURSTINE & OSBORN ■ client F. & M. SCHAEFER BREWING COMPANY

artist STEVE RANDOCK ■ art director JEFFERSON TESTER ■ agency LAWRENCE C. GUMBINNER
ADVERTISING AGENCY ■ client S. A. SCHONBRUNN & COMPANY, INC.

artist WALTER FRAME ■ art director NORMAN BYRON ■ agency BENTON & BOWLES, INC. ■ client THE BEST FOODS, INC.

41

42

artist RKO ART DEPARTMENT ∎ art director STANLEY SHERWIN ∎ client RKO RADIO PICTURES

YOU'LL GO FOR
COFFEE ICE CREAM SODA
WITH COFFEE ICE CREAM

artist JOSEPH BINDER ■ art director JULES MENGHETTI ■ agency J. M. MATHES, INC.
■ client PAN AMERICAN COFFEE BUREAU

Soup Makes The Summer Meal!

HEINZ *condensed* SOUP

HEINZ condensed CREAM OF TOMATO SOUP 57 VARIETIES MADE BY H.J.HEINZ CO.

57

■ artist GEORGE WASSBERG
■ art director M. KELLY
■ agency MAXON, INC.
■ client HEINZ

artist OTIS SHEPARD ■ art director OTIS SHEPARD ■ client WM. WRIGLEY JR. COMPANY

On its way to YOU

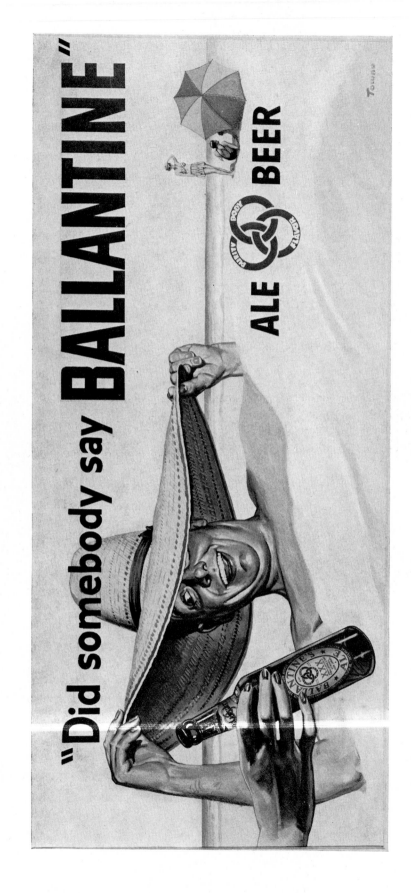

artist CHARLES TOWNE ■ art director JOHN A. COOK ■ agency J. WALTER THOMPSON COMPANY
■ client BALLANTINE BREWING COMPANY

artist ARMANT SEGUSO ■ art director STANLEY SHERWIN ■ client RKO RADIO PICTURES

RKO RADIO PICTURES presents

DOROTHY McGUIRE
GEORGE BRENT
ETHEL BARRYMORE

in

The Spiral Staircase

Kent SMITH Rhonda FLEMING Gordon OLIVER Elsa LANCHESTER

A DORE SCHARY PRODUCTION

SCREEN PLAY BY MEL DINELLI DIRECTED BY ROBERT SIODMAK BASED ON THE NOVEL "SOME MUST WATCH" BY ETHEL LINA WHITE

48

artist HOWARD SCOTT ■ art director HERBERT R. NOXON ■ agency McCANN-ERICKSON, INC.
■ client STANDARD OIL COMPANY OF NEW JERSEY

IN BOTTLES

AT FOUNTAINS

artist LOU CHAP ■ art director HARRY McGINNIS ■ agency NEWELL-EMMETT COMPANY ■ client PEPSI-COLA COMPANY, INC.

artist WINKLER-JEHLE ■ art director VINCENT TROTTA ■ agency NATIONAL SCREEN SERVICE
■ client PARAMOUNT PICTURES

50

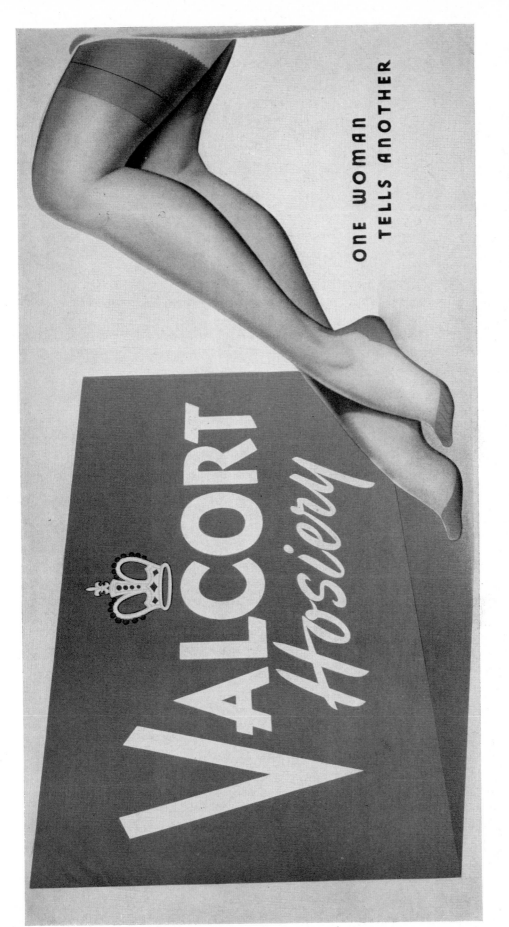

ONE WOMAN TELLS ANOTHER

VALCORT Hosiery

artist C. E. CORYN ■ art director HARRY J. JACKNICK ■ agency HARRY J. JACKNICK & COMPANY, INC. ■ client VALCORT HOSIERY CORPORATION

artist CARL PAULSON ■ art director JOHN A. COOK ■ agency J. WALTER THOMPSON COMPANY
■ client WARD BAKING COMPANY

a better beer *naturally* **Gretz** made the old-fashioned way—slowly... *naturally*

artist JOHN MILLIGAN ■ art director F. HOWARD SEBERHAGEN ■ agency SEBERHAGEN, INC.
■ client GRETZ BREWING COMPANY

artist MORGAN KANE ■ art director S. A. WELLS and W. C. SCOTT ■ agency McCANN-ERICKSON, INC.
■ client STANDARD OIL COMPANY-INDIANA

artist GLENN MACNUTT ■ art director AUGUST HIRSCHBAUM ■ agency ALBERT FRANK-GUENTHER LAW, INC.
■ client HAFFENREFER & COMPANY

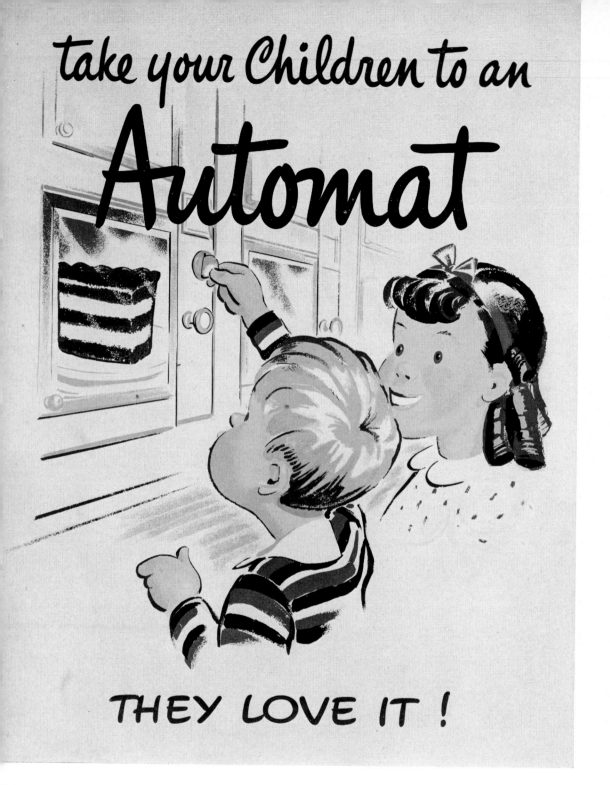

take your Children to an *Automat*

THEY LOVE IT !

artist WALTON S. THOMPSON ■ art director STANLEY F. SQUIRE ■ agency THE CLEMENTS COMPANY, INC.
■ client HORN AND HARDART

artist ROBERT O. REID ■ art director JAMES E. CLARK, JR. ■ agency CECIL & PRESBREY, INC.
■ client TOPPS CHEWING GUM

artist OTTO SOGLOW ■ art director JAMES E. CLARK, JR. ■ agency CECIL & PRESBREY, INC.
■ client TOPPS CHEWING GUM

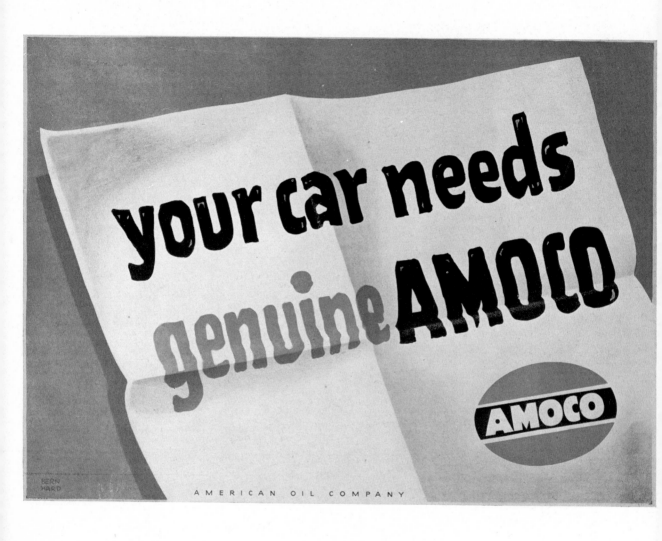

■ artist LUCIEN BERNHARD
■ art director GEORGE ADAMS
■ agency THE JOSEPH KATZ COMPANY
■ client AMERICAN OIL COMPANY

artist E. McKNIGHT KAUFFER ■ art director H. J. LAIRD ■ client AMERICAN AIRLINES, INC.

artist STANIFORD-SANDVICH ■ art director FRED GLAUSER ■ agency HONIG-COOPER COMPANY
■ client WINE GROWERS GUILD

artist STAHLHUT-HEINZERLING ■ art director GERALD LINK ■ agency KENYON & ECKHARDT

■ client KELLOGG COMPANY

artist **SARRA-BAUMGARDNER** ■ client NATIONAL FOUNDATION FOR INFANTILE PARALYSIS

artist ALBERT STAEHLE ■ art director HERBERT R. NOXON ■ agency McCANN-ERICKSON, INC.
■ client STANDARD OIL COMPANY OF NEW JERSEY

The following color plates printed from electros supplied by New York Subways Advertising, demonstrate how effective car card advertising can be when the artist is given the opportunity to tell his story in his own way.

These plates were selected from a series of beautifully designed miniature car cards produced under the direction of Mr. Jefferson Tester.

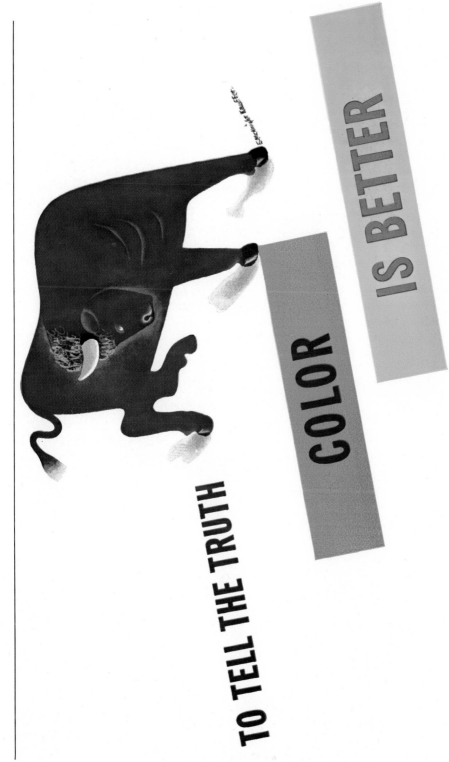

TO TELL THE TRUTH

COLOR

IS BETTER

artist E. McKNIGHT KAUFFER

artist ERIK NITSCHE

no hiding place down there:

every subway ad is in plain sight day and night

HUNGER ON WHEELS

Showing foods and drinks to millions of hungry and thirsty homeward bound New Yorkers daily, just when they want them most . . . this is Subway Advertising.

artist E. McKNIGHT KAUFFER

this is subway advertising

artist PAUL RAND

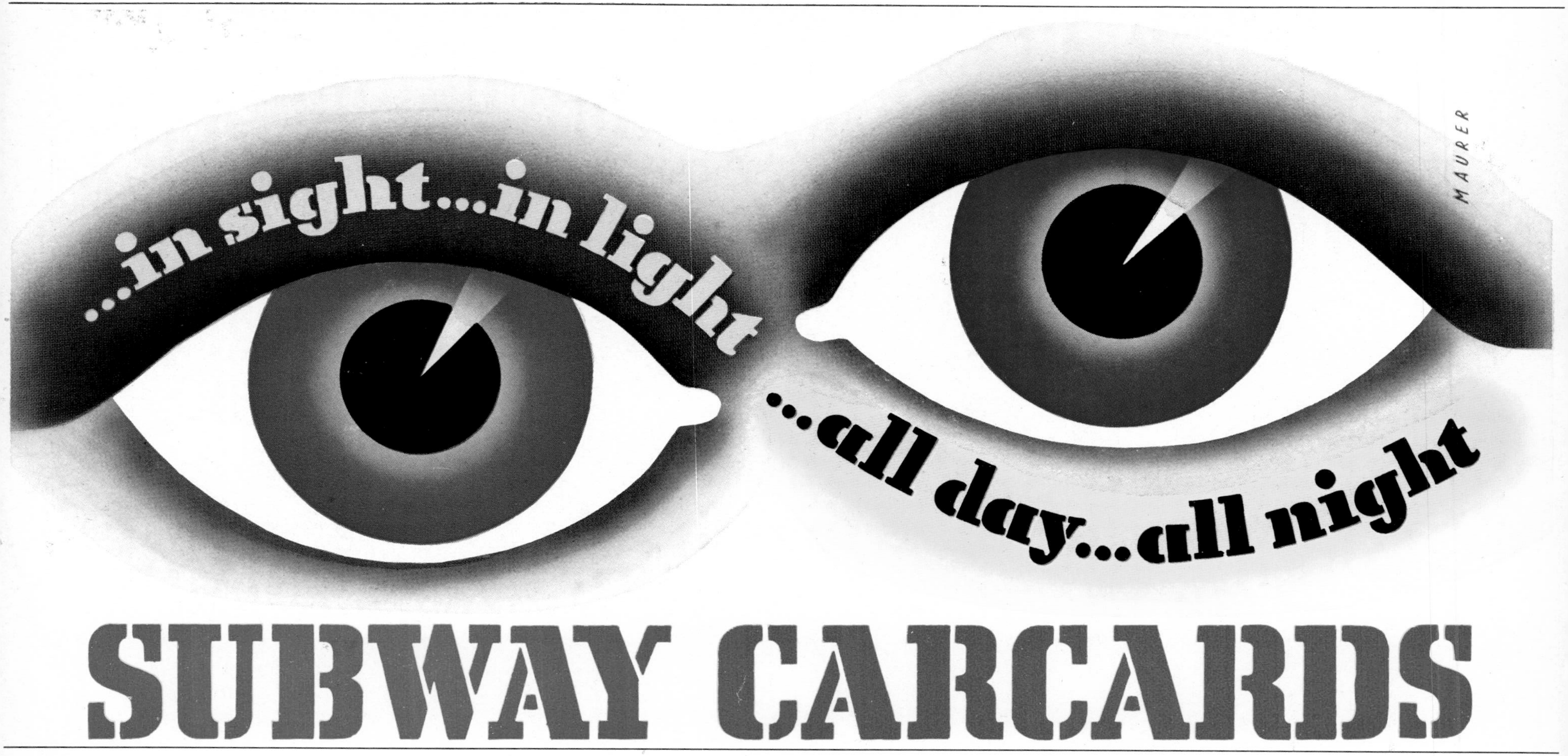
...in sight...in light
...all day...all night
MAURER
SUBWAY CARCARDS

artist SASCHA MAURER

LET US HAVE FAITH

 Books build character

LET THERE BE LIGHT

 Books broaden your horizon

...ON, SAIL ON!

 Books take you lands away

65

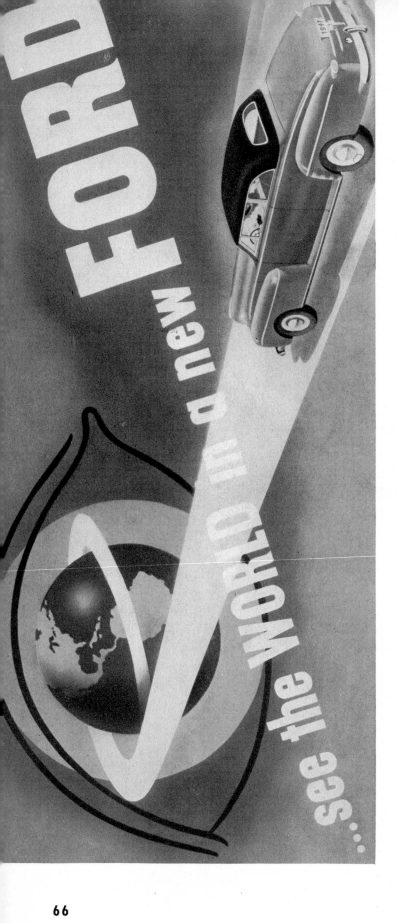

artist SASCHA MAURER ■ client McCANDLISH LITHOGRAPHING POSTER COMPETITION

66

artist KENNETH THOMPSON ■ art director PAUL SMITH ■ agency D'ARCY ADVERTISING COMPANY, INC. ■ client THE COCA-COLA COMPANY

Have a Coke

artist JIM NASH STUDIOS ■ art director WILLIAM JACOBY ■ agency NORMAN A. MACK AGENCY ■ client THE LIME COLA COMPANY, INC.

Simply Delicious

artist MAURICE LOGAN ■ art director CHARLES E. STANFORD ■ agency MILNE & COMPANY
■ client NALLEY'S, INC.

Get set for Winter...

WITH A TEXACO FALL CHECK-UP

artist LEO RACKOW ■ art director CHARLES E. MAHONY ■ agency BUCHANAN ADVERTISING ■ client TEXAS COMPANY

artist NORMAN JOLLIFFE ■ art director JACK SKOLNIK ■ agency PEDLAR & RYAN, INC.
■ client MILES LABORATORIES

Marchand's *Golden Hair-Wash*

— won't let time darken your hair!

artist MICHAEL ■ art director ERIC NICE ■ agency THE JOSEPH KATZ COMPANY ■ client THE CHARLES MARCHAND COMPANY

72

artist WILLIAM SEIFERT ■ art director DONALD S. JONES ■ client CONSOLIDATED EDISON

Surprising take-off

GULF

New NO-NOX Gas

artist HERBERT BOHNERT ■ art director WALTER GEOGHEGAN ■ agency CALKINS & HOLDEN
■ client GULF OIL CORPORATION

artist STAFF PHOTOGRAPHER ■ art director J. B. RICHARDS ■ agency MYER ASSOCIATES, INC.
■ client BURMA-VITA COMPANY

artist MORRIS SPINROD ■ art director DONALD S. JONES ■ client CONSOLIDATED EDISON

artist WM. E. ALLURED ■ art director WM. J. STRASSER ■ agency J. WALTER THOMPSON COMPANY
■ client FORD MOTOR COMPANY

FORD TRUCKS
LAST
LONGER

MORE FORD TRUCKS IN USE THAN ANY OTHER MAKE!

NEW ZEALAND
VIA PAN AMERICAN

artist P. G. LAWLER ■ client PAN AMERICAN WORLD AIRWAYS

artist P. G. LAWLER ■ client PAN AMERICAN WORLD AIRWAYS

artist E. McKNIGHT KAUFFER ■ art director H. J. LAIRD ■ client AMERICAN AIRLINES, INC.

artist P. G. LAWLER ■ client PAN AMERICAN WORLD AIRWAYS

artist P. G. LAWLER ■ client PAN AMERICAN WORLD AIRWAYS

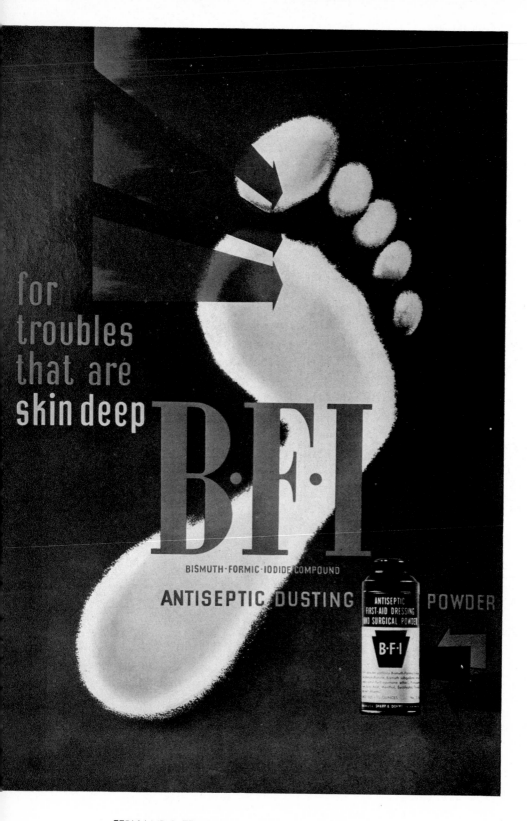

for troubles that are skin deep

B·F·I

BISMUTH-FORMIC-IODIDE COMPOUND

ANTISEPTIC DUSTING POWDER

artist FERNANDO TEXIDOR ■ art director MARTIN W. CARRICK ■ agency KETTERLINUS LITHO
■ client SHARP and DOHME

artist RIC HOWARD ■ art director GENE DAVIS ■ agency LA ROCHE & ELLIS ■ client ADAM HAT STORES, INC.

NORWAY   poster courtesy Scandinavian Airlines System

EGYPT   poster courtesy The Hamilton Wright Organization

Leksand

DALECARLIA · SWEDEN

SWEDEN   poster courtesy *Swedish News Exchange*

CANADA

poster courtesy *Province of Quebec Tourist Bureau*

poster courtesy Swedish News Exchange

poster courtesy *Air France*

MEXICO   *poster courtesy Mexican Tourist Association*

poster courtesy French National Railways

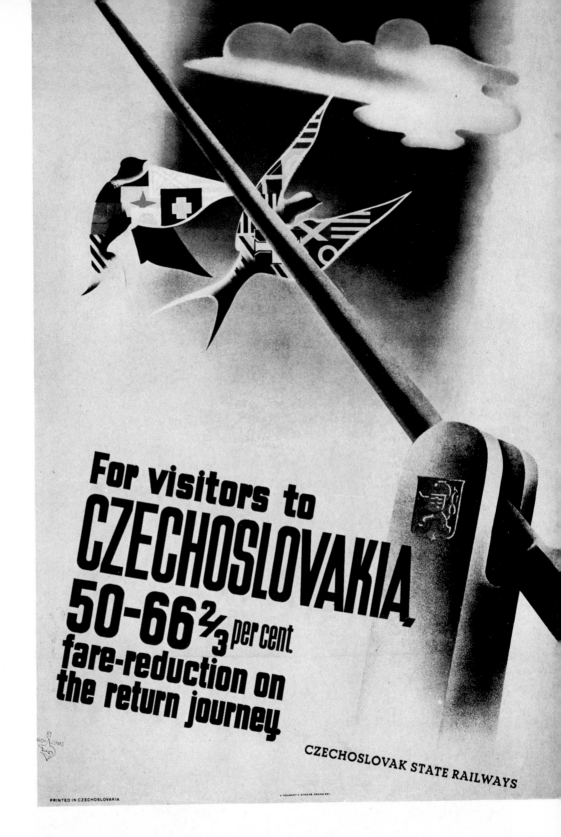

For visitors to
CZECHOSLOVAKIA,
50-66²⁄₃ per cent
fare-reduction on
the return journey

CZECHOSLOVAK STATE RAILWAYS

PRINTED IN CZECHOSLOVAKIA

CZECHOSLOVAKIA   *poster courtesy Czechoslovak Information Service*

SWEDEN

poster courtesy *Swedish News Exchange*

ENGLAND   *poster courtesy British Information Services*

poster courtesy Information Bureau of Uruguay

eat

A GOOD LUNCH

of at least:

milk
fruit or vegetable
protein
Canada approved bread

STRANKS

DESIGNED BY THE NATIONAL FILM BOARD FOR NUTRITION DIVISION · DEPARTMENT OF NATIONAL HEALTH AND WELFARE · OTTAWA, MAY , 1946

CANADA   *poster courtesy Canadian National Film Board*

SWITZERLAND   *poster courtesy* The Swiss Specialty Shop

MEXICO

poster courtesy Mexican Tourist Association

EGYPT   *poster courtesy The Hamilton Wright Organization*

INDEX OF ARTISTS

ARTIST	CLIENT	PAGE
NASH STUDIOS	*The Lime Cola Company, Inc.*	68
NITSCHE, ERIK	*New York Subways Advertising*	Color insert
OSBORN, ROBERT	*New York Subways Advertising*	Color insert
PATTERSON-HALL	*Wine Growers Guild*	31
PAULSON, CARL	*Atlantic Refining Company*	27
	Ward Baking Company	52
	Narragansett Brewing Company	32
PETERSHAM, MAUD-MISKA	*Children's Book Council*	18
POTTER-ZIEGLER	*Standard Oil Company-Indiana*	28
RACKOW, LEO	*Texas Company*	70
RAND, PAUL	*Community Committee*	16
	Cresta Blanca Wine Company	25
	New York Subways Advertising	Color insert
RANDOCK, STEVE	*S. A. Schonbrunn & Company, Inc.*	39
REID, ROBERT O.	*Topps Chewing Gum*	57
SANDVICH-STANIFORD	*Wine Growers Guild*	60
SARRA-BAUMGARDNER	*National Foundation for Infantile Paralysis*	62
SCOTT, HOWARD	*Standard Oil Company of New Jersey*	48, 64
SEGUSO, ARMANT	*RKO Radio Pictures*	47
SEIFERT, WILLIAM	*Consolidated Edison*	73
SHEPARD, OTIS	*Wm. Wrigley Jr. Company*	22, 45
SOGLOW, OTTO	*Topps Chewing Gum*	57
SPINROD, MORRIS	*Consolidated Edison*	76
STAEHLE, ALBERT	*Standard Oil Company of New Jersey*	63
STAHLHUT, HENRY	*Kellogg Company*	61
STANIFORD-SANDVICH	*Wine Growers Guild*	60
STANLEY, FREDERIC	*Standard Oil Company of New Jersey*	23
STEINWEISS, ALEX	*Columbia Recording Corporation*	24
	Schenley Distillers Corporation	35
SUNDBLOM, HADDON	*The Coca-Cola Company*	38
TEXIDOR, FERNANDO	*Sharp & Dohme*	84
THOMPSON, KENNETH	*The Coca Cola Company*	67
THOMPSON, WALTON S.	*Horn and Hardart*	33, 56
TOWNE, CHARLES	*Ballantine Brewing Company*	46
WASSBERG, GEORGE	*Heinz*	44
WHITE, NAT	*Gulf Oil Corporation*	29
WINKLER, ROY	*Paramount Pictures*	50
ZIEGLER-POTTER	*Standard Oil Company-Indiana*	28